PUBLIC

—— *poems* ——

Kevin Cadwallender

IRON PRESS

First published January 2001 by IRON Press
5 Marden Terrace
Cullercoats
North Shields
Northumberland
NE30 4PD
Tel/Fax: (0191) 253 1901
E-mail: seaboy@freenetname.co.uk

ISBN 0 906228 78 6

Printed by
Peterson Printers, South Shields

Typeset in Techno 12pt

Cover and Book Design by IRON Eye Design
@ IRON Press

Cover Photograph by Gilbert Johnston

IRON Press books are distributed by
Signature Book Representation Ltd
Sun House, 2 Little Peter St, Manchester M15 4PS
Tel: (0161) 834 8767
Fax: (0161) 834 8656)
E-mail: admin@signature-books.co.uk

northern arts
PROMOTING THE ARTS IN THE NORTH

SUPPORTED BY
THE NATIONAL LOTTERY
THROUGH
THE ARTS COUNCIL
OF ENGLAND

KEVIN CADWALLENDER is one of the best young poets writing in the North-East of England. Some poets call him 'the Captain'. Poet in Residence for the Cumbria Co-op in 1998, then Writer in Residence for The Great North Forest in 1999, as well as Poet in Residence at the Sunderland Echo newspaper in the Year of the Artist 2000. Kevin is well known for his performance poetry.
This is his first major collection, although the number of pamphlets he has published is legendary.
He runs the 'Origins' poetry and music performance venue in Newcastle and lives in Sunderland with Shabnam, Matthew, Niishani and Charlotte.

THANKS to:
Dave Calder, Kitty Fitzgerald, Peter Mortimer, Elle Ludkin, 'Legs' Bentley, Slim, Ginger and John Wesley as well as my family and other friends.

ACKNOWLEDGEMENTS

Some of these poems have previously appeared in the following:
Star Trek:the poems(IRON Press); Heterosexual Honkies (Wysiwyg Press) Baz Poems (Rebel Inc)
The Echo Room Yearbook, Smoke, Parasight, Portmanteau, Noises from the Isle, The Yonkly, A slow curve of liquorice, Croydon Poetry Festival Anthology, Ugly Light, Liquorice Root, Hardly Literature, Sons of Flint a & Pitch. Once Below a Time, Sunderland Echo, A Rumour of Tigers, Heartbreak Hotel, Baptism and The Captain's Log. Poetry Plus (Audio Cassette), In a City Art (Merlin films for Tyne Tees Documentary)

for John

Dedicated to Shabnam, Matt, Shani & Charlie

Contents

publisher's note:

The punctuation in this collection follows the express wishes of the author.

PUBLIC

Tom Jackson was fined twenty seven quid
for not scraping his dog's turd off the grass.

Janet Smithson pushes a bow bellied pram
over the shop window that is broken glass.

In the Catholic club protestants drink
empty bandits through security cages.

Terry Jones counts the cut the church will take,
last night was trouble free or so he judges

The boys outside the chippie are tribal,
they wolf whistle at the female moon,

The streetlights make it easier to sell drugs,
a shop doorway blurts a best selling tune.

and if I took the time to really look,
each one is a fiction in someone's book.

Chinese Johnny has won the pool tournament he is busy celebrating the lack of winner's grace he is known for; laughing like a drain as his victims fall empty pocketed into empty pockets; he rests his cigarette on the edge of the blue baize and mutters something inscrutable. The lads in the bar are forced to confront Johnny's own counterfeit stereotype as he whispers over cue balls swear words from asiatic brothels that he learned from wide-eyed phillipino girls in Singapore and Manilla;

Johnny speaks the vernacular of sailors, his skin is yellow, he speaks very little to the Japanese executives who drink without their wives in the lounge upstairs. He does not flinch or rise to the bait that his opponents proffer. "What part of Chinky do yer come from Johnny?" and when he replies "Hanoi" they never stop to think/argue/consider what part of the truth he is concealing from their puzzled white faces, contorted by alcohol and football results.

Spring has come early,
scraping the rust
from the supermarket trolley
daffodils shooting through mesh.
They walk dogs here all winter
and the worn trails are littered
with illegal shit.

Collecting
dandelion leaves
for salads,
an old woman
with a safeway carrier bag.

Spring has come early
and the men on the allotments
are removing cobwebs from hoes
and forks. Talking about rotivators
in the polythene shelters.

Selling seeds in the backroom

of the association shop.

Lifting the sneck, rusted to the painted gate.
I watch your eyelids opening as I push with clemmied boot.
You rise from a cracket like some ancient god,
All leather-skinned and billowing with tobacco twist.
Your pipe knocking on wood like a robin with a snail.
or at least; I remember your hopelessly happy voice
Singing between the rows
Where your cabbages have gone to seed.
I replace the sneck as I leave.
Hand the allotment keys over,
To the man who ignores the way
I grin at his sickle.

Ted Johnson died last night
clutching his glass at the bar of the British Legion,
Mourners shuffle to church
with their snuffles and bronchitis,
blame the change in the weather,
blame the cigarettes,
blame the colliery,
blame the war.

The shopping centre is full of widows,
Blue rinses in long out of season coats,
The check out operators are refusing old fifty pences,
saved in jars and lost in the backs of purses.
and
emptying

out from
the day centre,

'Mad Audrey'
is shouting
in Nordenham square,

"Jesus Loves me!"

Her dog barks like bedlam.

"I just kept seeing Jesus' hands, those blind palms",
She says this as she gazes through her own fingers, as if
hiding from something, something not quite darkness,
something like the fear of the lack of darkness, spiders
caught in their own webs, carapace covering nothing but
soft, unbroken silence.

"Just his hands, not a face, disembodied, damaged, trans-
fixed". I have heard they crucified through the wrists,
I read it in a book somewhere.
muttering as she leaves,
something about the Nazarene
and so many romans, so many romans.

The check out operator smiles
and takes payment for a tin of beans
in pennies raided from the now empty
Bell's whisky bottle.
She is bored and her tights

are making her sweat.
But her smile is a silver coin
in my copper life.
Me, I don't smile back
But I'd gladly exchange
my beans on toast
for a chance to lick the sweat
from every inch of her body.

*"Vous croiriez a l'approche de votre fin
Comme a la mienne"*

You would be right.

I drive my car through the streets everyday, I know them better than the back of my hand. I listen to old songs in an old car and think about poetry. It gets me from A to B. I walk when I do not have a car, I walk fast and keep my head down. I think about the new girl in the charity shop and the woman with one hand in the post office. When it rains I have a hood, when I am hungry I eat, when I am cold I buy coffee in Carricks. When I get tired I go home and telephone company.

...." the drugs don't work "

filters out from the open pub door
and flows down the pavement
carrying debris, sweet wrappers,
filter tips, betting slips.

the drugs do work
and keep us singing
in our chains.

This poet I know he's a teacher, right and he works all day and like he's got plenty of money but he isn't happy or anything and his lass is a teacher too and they go on long walks and he writes about trees and melancholy mostly and he doesn't know what to do with all those poems so I tells him you should be on the telly with all the other poets and he says poets don't go on the telly much and live like hermits and that, so I says what you doin' in a pub with me then and he just laughs and comes over all moody.

James doesn't know who I am,
He buys me a Stella Artois and fishes for my future,
he has a sixth sense, intuition, a third eye.
I don't like him much, I keep my mask on
when I am talking to him.

James has bought an Egyptian tarot pack,
I buy him cooking lager and show him my sinistral hand,
he makes a great show of avoiding eye contact
so that I think he knows something I don't.
I imagine him cutting his wrists.

James doesn't know who I am.
but I know who he is.
He's at the top of my list.
I lean across the table

rub the mark off his forehead,
he deserves all he gets

One day away from
the fourth seal.

The tree unclenches its gnarled wood fist
releases autumn onto the hardening earth,
dirty water swirling up through cracks
and changing dirt to mud.

The thrush drains opera into the red sky
relentless song and feathered mornings.
ugly light drips through from
the sun that is poisonous.

The sun that is ancient and impersonal,
all science burning through eyes
at the narrow ends of telescopes,
like god, too dangerous to ignore.

Love trapped in a heart for so long
pumping honey around arterial rhymes.
dissected, revealed as less than the rose,
cuts fingertips with jagged prose.

......and here comes Tom.
Barrel chested, ruddy faced,
Singing to himself
over the glare of the jukebox,

lyrics from a misheard song.

"Going down the bumpy hillside in your heavy hat!"

Tom doesn't recognise me as I slouch in
unshaven and order lager.
He greets me like a brother anyway.
When he remembers me he mentions
Coleridge as if he's some old mate of mine.
It's the only poet he has ever heard of.
The woman at the bar is a nurse, I know this.
Tom is under a curse, shitfaced in a state of grace,
Shouting in her face,
"Heal me, Heal me!"
When he really means "Save me"
Falling backwards into an empty net,
Tom shares his head with harpies;
harpies and regret.

Tom's mother in the launderette at night, saying
"I don't want to wash anyone's dirty linen in public, but.."

Harry is telling John about a knife fight
in Grampian Drive,
John doesn't believe him.
Later they will go to see the blood.
To verify the facts.

Harry and John are telling Rob about the blood
on the paving stones on Grampian Drive.

Rob says that it isn't Grampian Drive they mean
and that being a taxi driver he would know.

Harry would like to tell the girl in the wonder bra
about the knife and the blood, but now that Rob
has cast doubts on his geography, he can't.

John is telling the man behind the bar about
the blood on Grampian Drive.
Harry doesn't like the turn his rumour is taking.

Rob is telling a passenger in his taxi
about a knife fight that happened on Pennine Drive.
He has relocated the original myth.

The girl in the wonder bra is telling John about her tits.
John doesn't even mention the knife incident to her.
Later John will lick her out.
Harry is thinking about the blood on the pavement.
He checks it out on the way home.
Staggering , he re-enacts the last
moments of a dying man.
Slumps against the sign that says
'Grampian Drive'.
"Fucking knew it!"
he mutters.

John is coming in the girl with the wonder bra's mouth.

There was an old lady who swallowed a fly,
I don't know why she swallowed a fly,
Everyone dies. The littlest of deaths,

Snouting out through the soft crumble of soil. Cold air muzzled under half a moon on the trailing rose. Spun his body length from tip to tail. Welsh soil and blood and dust. New paint shading old. A thousand leather shoes trailing over territory. Thirst reached into his belly. He lapped at his eyes in the ancient shivering puddle. Memory; Old woollen cloth, tousled ash-taste of hair and the beer of a kiss. The see-saw of rabbit skin between tallstone and groundsel. Memory; hunting in the velvet of mole, a gate too tall for tongues where legs dangled like goose necks. Following the urgent nostalgia of him; Outside the singing house I waited to see the staggering out and happiness poured into my pitcher head. Him, in the stumble of words, who never leashed me. But tonight all the voices are not real. I am barking in mud on the dark estuary. There is an empty place like something buried and forgotten. He wells up inside of me like rain. Poetry does not smell of anything worth digging. I wait in the shade and growl at mice.

Dylan sits in 'The Strawberry',
tells stories about whores on Pink Lane
in the good old days when booze was as
cheap as blow jobs down the backalley-
windfall nights on cobbled back Stowell
where the poets come out to piss
and glue is the currency of communication.

Caitlin dancing Duncanesque
down the Cloth Market with the boys in white
open necked shirts and the white-legged bait
giggling up secret streets and in and out of the
archways near the Castle Keep.

here is a secret for all the bull necked children
rutting out their days on the revolving dancefloors
and puking over the side of Gateshead tied princesses.

here is a dog barking on a housing estate at
helicopters circling overhead like dragonflies.
The punctuation of nothing.
The lager-priested shorelines.
Madly baying beneath
a Briggflatts moon.
Buggerall backwards.

Julie and Debbie and Sharon
knocking back two for the price of one
Moscow Mules on the Tuxedo Royale.

Gazing out over the quayside
at the mull and madness.
Julie whispers heresy
into the brown ale waters.

"I've had enough of this shit!"

Debbie and Sharon, dull eyed

nod in mute agreement.
Dance to old songs
with automatic steps.

Watching the waters of Tyne
emptying out of their veins
like a slow suicide.

The ghosts of past conquests come back to haunt me, Cleary in his broadest brogue and grin, "Would you take a run at her, Kevin?'

When Harry met Debbie
she sucked his cock in the cinema
while he thought of coming in
Meg Ryan's mouth.

She imagined he tasted
like Tom Cruise although he
looked more like Billy Crystal
in the shifting blue of the screen.

His parents were rich.
Her parents were dead.
University was about the
only thing they had in common;

except perhaps, banality.

Dancing now, through some

'Blondie' song because
'Debbie Harry'
was like an omen
scrolled in lipstick on
the mirror in
the ladies lavatory.

If I believed in the rhetoric of apathy; If I believed that we all end up transfixed by the ugly light. If I believed in anything at all, then that would be enough to rob me of true belief.

Make this public
if you can.

Sailing out of Eden's open mouth,
The seedlings of tall ships;
Carrying scar memories of
Fallen timber.
The detail of the wind,
blows leaves in the heads of trees.
History's fingers point
Centuries into tense.
Recording against ghost Sycamore
The rip-saw of policy.
Plantations of Oak;
Growing new hearts
To the crackle of burning elms;
Orange with disease.

An old man
His face young against bark
walks a slow dog.

Tall trees tell tales
Of children;
Sailing out of
Eden's mouth.

Drowning in bird song.
The land smells of wild garlic.
We pick our way clumsily
Over the crackling trail.

A hallmark of civilisation;
Our lack of stealth.
Finding; finally a path
Constructed for us.
We are unparadised.
In the beck; a supermarket trolley
Erodes into the rusty evening.

Knowing neither the names of flowers;
Nor their nature. We breathe in communion.
Inspire God without faith.

The housing estates peeping-tom at lovers
With a head for heights. Their initials
Branded on the big branched oak.
Tattered carrier flags; banner litter trees

Ticker-tape parades in canopies of green.

This celebration of senses;
Each blurred leaf a Seurat.

Arthritic tree knuckles;
Cramped tight; Fist-wood.
Clenched at the sky.
We limp through the Dene
In ill fitting reverence and footwear.
Randy as tourists for souvenirs.
Picture-postcard gloss; snapping like
Cameras over humus-boned carpets.
A bloodshot sun beating out veins
In the night-skinned sky.
A slow swing wrings the neck of a bough.
Too heavy for childhood we drink
The creaking day away.
Drawn by heady seasons;
We come here with friends
To be alone.

Nursing feral dreams in tamed heads.

Each Summer's walk
A passing.   Of sorts.

In rigid waves; teeth bite the skyline.
A rush of geometry to the senses.
Stunted squares and empty flagpoles.

Cars in row upon row;
Secured and alarmed
Against consenting adults;
Who breach the tranquil apathy
Of a town desperate for a heart.

A maze of straight lines
And dead ends with taxi drivers;
Going round in circles
For mathematical improbabilities.

In slow deliberate shoals;
The shoppers fill their lives
With frozen food and tabloid answers.

Heading home; these tin men and women;
To personal landscapes of debt
And weekend dancing.

and if I could be bothered to take a look
each one of us is a fiction in some one else's book.
and if I could be bothered to take a look
and if I could be bothered
and if I could
and if.............

LOVE ON A BRANCH LINE

on the metro, rab says he's in love with
the woman who says, "Mind the doors,Please"
i tell him it's a machine but he's smitten anyway.
as he leaves the train he knows he'll maybe never
hear that voice again, he knows he'll always
'Mind the doors' cos she's stuck in his head
like the lord's prayer, like the ten times table,
like an ice pick.
we board another train but the voice is a man
a man who doesn't ken rab, who rab doesn't love
and he pines for her gentle reassurance and certainty.
but she's unfaithful and like an answerphone
hopelessly attentive to duty. she is breaking poets'
hearts up and down the east coast line. with a
poet in every terminus and her limited vocabulary.
rab says the tyne bridge is beautiful at sunrise and i
can see regret, pulling the emergency cord,
inverting timetables, return ticketing him
back to newcastle in winter, when she'll be there
consistent if repetitious, and finding her at last
re-enacting ' strangers on a train '.
pulling in to glasgow central julie says
there must be a woman somewhere that made
that recording. but there's no romance in that,
there's no romance in the attainable, it's only
when you think it can never happen, that it happens.
and rab's love is pure. it is not tainted by flesh,
he is not enthralled by just lust; this is spiritual,
this is disembodied, like a poem outside of a poet,

like the speaking clock, it's nothing personal,
it's nothing rational.
julie, is finishing her white wine and slipping
between tired sheets.
rab has a voice in his head like the clear white light
and soon he'll be calling out her name
and talking in tongues.

TRUE COLOURS

Tracy has two babies; one black, one white,
she calls them her own private 'toon' army.
takes them to sit in the stands.
one of them was once kissed by Kevin Keegan
on a day when the press were invited.
Tracy spends her benefit on season tickets
and 'babygros'. Breast feeds behind the
opposition goal, has a tattoo on her wrist
of a magpie, collects autographs like silver paper,
precious little names glued on the walls of her nest.
waiting for the landlord to come and fix the gas fire.
decided her kids would be better off in the care
of rugby union supporters. Left a scribbled note;
black biro on white and two kids wrapped in a
hand-knitted scarf in away colours.

JULIAN AND THE OCCULT

Julian is a Witchfinder General.
He works at 'Pets 'R' Us',
stalking all the demons
who talk to cats and
buy their familiars gifts.

Cutting a swathe in his Hopkin's hat.
a birch rod swishing through the aisles.

At night he interrogates
the mute snakes,
the evil hamsters wet
from his miniature ducking stool.
Scoops the floating fish
from the hubble bubble of tanks
proclaims them innocent.

Once he told me
over non-alcoholic lager,
that he'd seen the great Satan
shopping for souls in Sainsburys
where Julian has a part time job
stacking shelves on the nightshift.

"When do you find time to sleep"
I ask him.
He looks at me like
I've masturbated in church,
A cruel sneer twisting his lips,

Crying, "Sleep! Sleep!
Evil never sleeps,
Evil never sleeps."

LISTEN, LISTEN

Listen,Listen, I'm trying
but your minimalism escapes me,
that one about the field of dead cows
which doesn't mention fields or cows,
lost me off in the first stanza,
I understand your concerns,
what was it you were muttering?
something about the purity of your art,
something about the radicalisation of
experimental form, something about the
image being all and the manifesto
of realism being redundant.

Listen, Listen, I'm trying but it seems to me
you were too concerned with form
and missed the life-form that was
desperately trying to attract your
attention with body language that
even a regional poet like me
could translate at forty paces
with myopic binoculars.
and while we are on the subject
do you really believe that life
is subordinate to art or was that just
a pose? and no, I didn't know that
Ezra Pound was the only poet apart
from yourself who never recanted
in the face of charges of obscurity,
but it doesn't surprise me, Buddy boy,
and before you launch into your

next sparkling critical theory
get your fat arse to the bar
and get the Guinness in.

Yes I'm sure it's your round.
I am a realist.

PUGILISM

Got some boxing gloves one christmas
and a punch ball, red leather, knocked hell out of it,
it never hit back.
Me and Kenny, one afternoon
had a boxing match,
same christmas present, see.
we sparred and lightly tapped each other,
he jabbed me once or twice, nicked my cheek
with rough sewn seams.
We floated like butterflies for a bit
and then he stung me like a bee
and opened up a lightning gash
under my left eye, with a hammered
home fist full force and followed up
with a lethal combination
that left my nose spread
across my face all blood and snot.
I went fuckin' light
and pummelled him
with outrageous roundhouses
with him saying sorry and
putting his guard up to fend me off.
A sort of cross between
Raging Bull and Tommy Steele's
Little White Bull.
I flailed until he pinned
me with a left hook
that put me down
and counting backwards
in frustration.

I swapped my gloves for a subbuteo.

Kenny got put in Borstal for knifing his Dad.

THE BUILDING TRADE

Julian is a existentialist. he works on a building site
with Tom the labourer, Fred the brickie and Bob the hod
carrier.
it works like this; Tom fills Bob's hod up with bricks,
Bob carries them to Fred and Fred builds a wall.
Julian's job is to help the bricks understand their own
reality.

Tom has ham sandwiches for lunch, Bob has cheese and
Fred has egg.
Julian doesn't eat lunch as he feels this is saying 'no'
to a society which insists on social imperatives such as
lunch.
Sometimes the bricks argue with Julian saying
"but we have the right to freedom"
Julian smiles, " man is condemned to freedom"
"but we are bricks" they cry, "why do you oppress us?"
some days the walls just don't get built at all.
Julian doesn't sleep well.
he dreams of a mass uprising of bricks,
of boundaries collapsing all over suburbia,
of Sunday morning street warfare with flymos
and hovers clashing over disputed inches of turf,
of middle class landowners with nothing to keep
their mortgages in.......
secretly,
Tom practises hod carrying
Bob practises bricklaying
and Fred is doing a nightclass in sociology.
Julian is an existentialist and lives outside

of the restrictions placed upon him by the
constant problem of having no self to esteem
and no self to be 'ish' with
this however does not prevent his sleeping
with the gaffer's daughter who has
a B.tec in Freudian hairdressing,
which means that everytime
she cuts someone's hair
they look like a dick.

WRITER'S WORKSHOP

I took it clunking and steaming into the workshop,
told him, "I'm thinking about trading it in on a newer model" He gave it the
once over, tutted like a metronome and smiled,"God, I haven't seen one of
these for years!" "It's a classic" I told him. "An English Sonnet with three
quatrains and an underslung rhyming couplet."
"That may well be so" he rallied, "but the scansion is shot to buggery, the
couplet isn't firing on all syllables, the metre's showing signs of unstress
and one of your similes has slipped out of tense"
So I say,"But can you fix it?"
And he just grins and says , "Well I could but it'll cost yer! Y'see it's the parts
they just don't make them anymore and the ones that are made out of kits
are just sub-standard"
"Still" he says, "I'll get my mate to have a look,
He's got an old Petrarchan which might just have some bits we could
cannibalise".... "you can borrow that old Villanelle to get you home,"
"No thanks", I say, "I've got a friend to pick me up in his cut and shut prose
convertible, I'll pop in tomorrow".....
"What's the damage" I sez ,Two months later.Well he sez,
"There's some good news and some bad.....We've had to lose

the metaphor completely so we've welded together a couple of conceits from
an old Donne Metaphysical , We've had to assonate the rhyme scheme,
realign the pentameter and transfer an epithet to get it started at all, but if
you don't mind chugging along on re-tread cliches she'll go for a few years
yet.
I thanked him, payed the outrageous reading fee
and decided it might have to be retired from competition or brought out as a
party piece when people accuse me of being a Monologue enthusiast with
too much irony in my unleaded pencil.

BANDITS AT ONE O'CLOCK

for alec
it is always bandits at one o'clock.
after the queue in the temple
after the post office
identification tattered
after the first pint of caffrey's.

the barrels roll.

folding money translates into tokens
tokens translate into two things
beer and no beer.
the dart board does not have the same
ambiguity.
the pool table plays for bigger cash;
heavier losses.

at the bookies
alec follows the shoal.
each way.

it is always bandits at one o'clock
and at three
short red pens
and rich men's horses.

RED TREVOR

I have bought books from him before
and fish.
His carrier bag is legendary in the bar.
the last book he sold me
was
'Field, Factories and Workshops Tomorrow'
by Peter Kropotkin.
Trevor says
the end is good
but the theory is dodgy.

I ask for kippers
he talks about
his dogma
as if it means something.

I am only interested in hunger.
he talks about 'mutual aid'
and inventive genius.

I buy us both a drink.
We watch the same football match
on the same television,
His side is losing.
He will not admit it.

He promises me fish
next week and more books
many more books.

LIQUORICE ROOT

susan harris had liquorice legs
red in woolly tights and skinny
like sapling branches
i chewed on a knuckle of
root, unscrewed from the
jar next to aniseed balls
and kop-kops.
me with my school tie
askew and brylcreemed up
for photographs
she said
kiss, cuddle or torture
and i in suave gob smacked
reply said kiss although
she didn't and wouldn't
not even when bribed
with promises of penny arrows.

some kids got kissed
by anybody. mothers and
fathers and even susan harris.
i was saving my lips
for the catholic girl
who had red hair and a
green hat although the
reverend cole said i'd
have to be confirmed
to get into heaven and
into the church christmas
party.

david cormack used to tell
us stories about his sister
until we grew clothes pegs
in our khaki shorts
i used to dream about her
but never found out
what to do with
clothes pegs until
later and by then
david cormack's sister
used to buy nappies
at the co-op.

farmer crystal never let us
play on his field he said his
bull was dangerous and would
kill us but we knew
he would kill it
and make beef and
all the cows too.

stealing flowers off
graves for mother's day
and cigarettes from
the paper shop was not
the same thing.
mam always liked the flowers
but we didn't always like the cigarettes.

the student teacher

in year one used to inhabit
my dreams,
i rolled an old penny
to her one day in art
and she called me a stupid boy.
after that
i was unfaithful.

when barry venners
stole my bike
he was kind
enough to
give me a ride
home first
so i was sad
to hear that he'd
got killed
under a bus
and told his dad so
when he
brought my bike
back.

my dad wouldn't
let me have an air rifle
but kenny bell had one
so we shot all the birds
out of the trees and
practiced funerals.

jenny dove had a lovebite
off george cowan
so we said she'd had it
and exchanged knowing looks.
but she took off her jumper
once and we looked at
her nipples .
i dreamt about
jenny dove that night
and woke up sticky

school blazers i found
are not ideal for putting
out fires in bramble bushes.
they can't keep secrets and
tell your mam that somebody
somewhere has been smoking
even when they weren't.

saying loudly
during assembly
our father which farts in heaven
used to be more fun when i was
little. god, they warned, knew
everything and was everywhere
and i thought he'd be more
offended by what dad said
when my sister spent the
night in a tent with
trevor cartwright

and came home all ruffled
like a haystack.

the worst thing about
being a little boy
is that no one listens
to you except other little
boys who don't bother to pick
you when it comes to football.
and little girls who say
they like you one minute
and the next minute
they run off to singapore
cos their dad's in the army
and never give you back
the comics you lent them
and grow up into strangers
on buses when you haven't
had a wash and want to talk
to them and
god not listening
and p.e. teachers
and liking liquorice root.

THERE ARE PLACES WHERE IT IS NOT SAFE TO DANCE.

Snow on Liberty Island. Some tarnished goddess in Reeboks with a torch for tourists. Cold water on its way to Cuba and the air pretzel heavy with salt. All this culture. Kerouac never met Mayakovsky but here in this downtown train the charges are laid.An American rat moves between tracks under Manhattan megaliths. It is raining on Fifth Avenue, wet Easter and damp Passover; In the 'White Horse' sheltering from the onslaught of poetry; from the waiters in plimsolls. Exchanging travellers cheques for cigarettes in a Coney Island Deli, The man behind the counter gives me change in broken English. The homeless are in rehearsal on each block their lines are linked somehow to the prayers that go straight up to Mammon on Wall Street. Everybody is a statistic of some description. A girl on the subway danced for a dollar.

There are places where it is not safe to dance.

The cemetery on a hot afternoon is guarded by security men with pistols. The dead sleep peacefully, safe as American footprints on the Moon. Clutching a broken suitcase in Grand Central Station; Clinging to a bottle of lager in J.F.K. I have all the souvenirs I need to alter my perceptions.

CHEZ NAZI

Digging the red soil,
Adolf tends the garden
in polyester slacks and golf shoes,
Wagner drifting from the shiny CD
Pruning the roses from the weeds
he is content.
These days he is not so intense,
keeps his megalomania in a box
with the medals he awarded himself
and a lock of Eva's hair.
He is a good gardener.
All mass murderers have beautiful
gardens, bones and blood make a
good basis for growth.
I see him in the garden centre
pricing bird tables and furniture.
He seems happy.
But it's strange
since he moved in
next door our flowers
don't look the same,
they're tall and strong
but they never last the summer,
their petals wilt and their stalks
lie like memories on compost.
Clean shaven these days and
dabbling in watercolours
I watch his stooped figure
raking over the ashes
of a bonfire

ANARCHY IN THE U.K.

Swapping your bondage trousers
for the articles of a law you could not endorse,
was not the brightest spanner you ever threw into the
works.
Now we sit in silence.
You tell me to watch your coat
as you go for a slash.
"Someone might steal it"
you inform me.
I dredge a memory from the back catalogue
of your convictions.
and
think you are right
Someone might.
Ten years ago it might have been you.

JUDAS' CHARIOT

What the fuck you on about?
Judas never had a fucking chariot!
Never had fuck all except ready cash.
D'yer really think he'd barter?
Give us the king o' the Jews
an' we'll give yer anything yer like.
Alright. I've always fancied a chariot.
No man, he kissed Jesus on the cheek
betrayed with a kiss do yer not read yer scripture?
No it wasn't a bit like your ex-lass
She betrayed you with a fuck.
No, I don't want to see your appendix scar ,
I believe yer.

CALLOUS IN SUNDERLAND

Walking the Chester Road
with you shouting maliciously
"You arrogant bastard!"
made me feel as if I was
about to be written out
of a soap opera
and
when you slapped my face,
I was surprised how much
it didn't hurt and that the
sound created was not quite
in synch
and might have to be dubbed
later.
I mouthed my scripted apology;
you played Greta Garbo and
melodrama.
I opted for bathos;
our ratings went through the roof.

god, how you would have laughed,
opening this letter from a passer-by
who imagines we are real.

Much later we made love,
although I was using a
stunt double for the
tricky orgasmic bit.

THE TEMPEST

Caliban Edwards the worse for twenty years of drink
really believes that this barmaid who has heard it all
before is the one for him. Lurches up and orders one
for the road, gabbles out some perfunctory remark
before slipping out to the take away and the usual
clammy hand under the duvet.
and love is a forlorn hope
in this grubby little world
and why bother with romance
when you don't know the steps
to this erroneous dance.
Miranda Richards clears away the debris
catches a taxi to her mother's ideal home,
lies awake thinking of all the flotsam that
floats on the head of a gallon of drink, tells herself
that amongst the drips who gather around the drip
trays there must be one who is special, closes her eyes
thinks about a jacket in dorothy perkins' window.
and love is a mystery to itself
it is unable to contemplate how
low it has fallen and like every
precious commodity depreciates
in the passing of days.
Ferdinand Jenkins has a fax and a mobile phone
writes love letters to strangers on the internet,
books a bucket seat for a desperate fortnight
on some god forsaken island.

YAKIMA OUTHOUSE

Slanted wood falling into bare Winter pine.
Carver's fingerprints on cold metal handle.
Pressed snow trail over broken fence fragments.
These are lines of reference , for the man.

A shrine for dirty realism then?
I can picture the graduates rolling up,
eager cameras; posing in inappropriate
haute cuture for another writer to
cross off their experience lists.
I remember my own voyeurism
in the White Horse Tavern,
I tell myself because I can,
"go back to writing
  about your own
  life",
this is a stranger's fiction.

Cukes, String Beans, Okra,Huckleberries,
Cots, Sweetcorn, Cants, Squash,Spuds.

I know what they are
but I cannot savour the taste.

Slanted wood leaning into top heavy Silver Birch,
My own Yakima outhouse where I kept rabbits,
Worn out grass pathway avoiding white dog turds.
My lines of reference, this man, this day, this life.

I drink but have never reached the edges of my drinking.
She tells me “I’m too human to be a great writer”.

Ray has the same look as Tess in the last
two pictures of the book I am closing.

CHEZ GUEVARA

slumped in front of the tv
riddled with bulletins
from the latest armed coup.
Wondering if that razor blade
in the bathroom is sharp enough
for one last close shave.

khaki underwear drying,
faded camouflage for
the play station photo shoot.
a walk on role in Evita
in the west end and then
a poster in the Athena
end of season sale.

feeling less than legendary.
eyes full of bluebottle larvae.

Someone, somewhere
has disconnected the
revolution.

HOKUM JUNKIES

Reading tarot cards and
chanting mantras on wet beaches
got us nowhere.
and Moonchild's flashback to
her previous existence as
Cleopatra's pedicurist gave
us bad karma that all our crystals
and homeopathy couldn't counter.
and you babbling on about
Chakra Khan and the joke
about the Korma Sutra
not being on the menu
were just more kitsch
on the road to Nirvana.
Although the local freesheet
made us a headline the Dalai Lama
would have eaten a chicken for;
"I-chinging in the Rain"

RADICAL

It's about time we had this out in the open,
us being brothers under the skin
the number of cars congregating in your drive,
the way you call a living room a lounge,
the way we still talk about revolution
but you spend your weekends at Ikea,
the way your cheques never bounce,
the way you talk about careers and the
future as if you've lost faith in barricades,
the uneasy tilt of your brown ale
as you tell me that idealism is for the young,
the way you've moved on,
and all the important things we used
to rage at and rail against are all viewed
through a telescope as if we never spray
canned anything on a wall or never marched
singing through the streets or never believed
anything was possible.
You tell me
I should grow up.
Stop being angry at the world.
Get into Star Trek
and barbecues.
Say
'God, I remember giros!'
like they'd gone out of fashion
or worse have become
an embarrassment you

never share with anyone
at the office and only
in the past tense
with old friends.

MAROONED

for Seema

That summer was haywire;
a battered maroon volkswagon
and 'the Rye' blistering our
way to Dillon's doorstep.
Heavy headed in the 'Diggers',
we sold our wedding bands
and burned the certificate
in a stainless steel sink.

Now, we grow cosy out of choice;
exchanging vows in private,
Turning into the family we
always hoped for but guarded against.

Drinking alone
like the old days,
I no longer feel the pull of movement,
Finding inertia desirable in the
tracing of your spine.

I tear the back off a beermat
and write your name carefully,
I don't want to get it wrong.

MOSCOW COWBOYS

gunfight at the boris yeltsin corrral.
red stars and sigue sigue sputnik.
she's line dancing in lenin's tomb,
drinking like a cossack
at a macdonald's drive-thru.

and all the moscow cowboys
are drinking budweiser
posing in levi's
and swapping
soviet brown bear hats
for stetsons.

COOKING KIPPERS FOR THE CAT

Dave is cooking kippers for the cats,
In the debris and the penance of his flat.
And making coffee, once more for me
as I ponder under the purring of fleas
this scrum of backs.
The smoked smell of fish
alerts this squadron of cat-napping,
bird-snatchers and mice-biters,
They synchronise their movements
and wrap themselves round legs
like fur puttees.

I flick through a tired copy
of Pickard's 'Jarrow March',
Target a particular point
on the floral patterned wallpaper
with my watch face.
Tease the kitten out of an old cat.

Gone now....
With the advent of cloud.
A whip of tail betrays frustration.

Nothing changes much.
The imperceptible march of days.
Grey faced marchers in a poet's book.

Going down to London
to look at the Queen

JULIAN AND THE FINAL FRONTIER

Julian is a Klingon 'bird of prey' pilot,
He studies I.T. at the university,
he speaks several languages
all of them are from Star Trek!

In the summer he signs on
citing as his preferred occupation;
Pilot: cloaked or uncloaked.

The D.S.S. supervisor has bought
an English/ Klingon Dictionary.
She is learning how to say
"suspended from benefits"
but for now she leans across
the counter and says,
"do KHA"
which means,
"That is unfortunate".

Julian duly amends his form
to 'anything in computers.'
(Borg and Cardassian empire excluded)
How far he is willing to travel
depends on the warp capacity of his 'wessell',
a clapped out Ford Fiesta
bought via the internet from
the Ferrenghi Chemistry student
at Manchester University.

Julian got a job at McDonalds

where he is an extra, waiting
to be beamed off the planet's surface,
uses his expertise to teach the
customer service droids
the perfect Vulcan death grip.

JUST ANOTHER BEACH POEM

The sea has been
told to stay behind
and writes endless
lines on an empty beach.

A seagull's wing
beaten by death
fans sand across
lucky horseshoes.

The sun is still
the same busy bodying
old schmuck,
head in clouds.
Cutting up rough
on pink podgy thighs.

Ice cream jerks off
Onto bland pavement.
Punch and Judy
with those new
social conscience puppets;
The community worker
and The Relate counsellor.

The sea acts out its daily ritual,
Moons around in wet dreams.

A coin in a slot will buy you everything
but what you need.

SHIELDSMAN

All aboard the 'Freda Cunningham'
for 40 pence worth of Tyne.
Across the ribbed waters
between Shields;
Seagulls trawling meat.
Scuppered by real ale in the 'Alum House'
We exchange timetables for tidal dreams,
Drink to the ghostly whores of the 'Northumbria'.
Saluting the new age sailors hiding
in the flannel petticoats of
this weeks 'Dolly Peel'.

Sailing all my Nine to Fives
on a couple of miles of Tyne;
Captain of my office and the typing pool,
I shanty, thirsty as a dry dock to the 'Chain Locker'
Drowning in the backwash of my favourite brew.
I am lost with all my shanghaied shipmates.
Peering out at the silent cranes;
Fishing for boats in the half-light,
After all the boats are gone.
My children are bred on new words.

Revitalisation. Refurbishment. Redevelopment

They pose on the quayside in Adidas and Reebok trainers.
'Coke' in hand as if they were put on the streets by
An executive in charge of product placement.

Reclamation.   Rejuvenation.   Redundancy

Wangling the last jingle out of the Income Support;
Young mothers head for the bright lights of South Shields.
Watch their kids wasting time on the same
phantomless ghost trains,
the same gaudy taste of candy floss
sticking the future into place.
Heading home
after being sick on the beach after
one too many revolutions
on the 'Traum boat'
or one too few at home.
All aboard the 'Shieldsman'
We sat tired and sea-legless
singing 'Water of Tyne' in
tuneless harmony.

Watching anchors rust in the iron twilight.
Hardly able to grasp where it had all gone.

SCRAPING STARS OFF BROADWAY

Under your feet
and picking your pockets
and armed and dangerous
and hungry for fame and
black and white and ugly
and beautiful and preaching
on subways and littering
the streets and dancing
for quarters and singing
for dimes and professionally
disabled and moles in the
lower levels of Hell and this
country of city-size cemeteries
and dreamers and pretzels
and culture raking the gutters
and old men playing poker
at midnight and lost tourists
and strange chocolate and
sheer, grinding poverty and
sheer, grinding wealth and
the noise of car horns and
the quiet cathedrals and the
all night delis and the crack
of sidewalk and the height
of liberty and the Bronx is up
but the Battery's run down
and dead presidents and film
stars. The edges of everything
blur and the Guide on a
Central Park Horse and trap.

outside of the Dakota building
hollering,
"This is where they shot
Rosemary's Baby and
John Lennon."

BAZ AND THE BOURGEOISIE

in her lounge, like she didn't have a living room
and Baz rattling on about how he never scabbed
and me feeling guilty for not being a miner
and the Austrian crystal decanter getting
more and more offensive and the imitation pit lamps
were just as stuck up as her gobshite of a husband
who droned on and on about his shares in British Gas
and how his Procol Harum LPs were so bastard rare
it didn't matter if they were crap or not.

And me being polite as usual and nodding
in all the right places and Baz
wanking the West Highland White
under the table with his boot
and bolting Mousakka and Bull's Blood and tryin'
not to look down the low cut dress of our gracious host
who reckons her and her significant other
have an 'open relationship',
from the 'Open university'.
and me feeling like a killjoy puritan
as Baz reckons he's scored and comes
up grinning from under the table
like some perverse synchronised swimmer.

and I can't find my car keys
and now 'Gerard' is showing me his
'Star Wars' airfix kits and trying to put
his hand on me bum
and Baz I can tell is shagging noisily
like a bollock in a china shop,

the crystal decanter chatters nervously.

and I'm out of there,
Baz trailing, cursing
tripping over his libido
as it pulls its kecks up.

Halfway home Baz eyes me suspiciously,
"you're a bit of a snob aren't yer, Kev"

and reluctantly I have to agree.

ROCK'N'ROLL *(I gave you the best years of my life)*

True, I could never play guitar like Chuck Berry
or duck-walk without severe embarrassment and
a chiropractor on stand-by, Yet I stuck with you.
Bought my singles recklessly with no thought
for the future of vinyl, bought them with pay
packets and giros and when I was skint
sold them at a loss
to feed myself.
True when the sixties became psychedelic
I could never bring myself to wear all those tie-dye
shirts and loons and when 'San Francisco'
was the place to be I was paralytic in
a 'Yates' wine lodge in Blackpool
but what the Hell!
It was the only west coast I could afford
and Kerouac's mysticism would have been lost on me
the only out-of-body-experience I ever had
concerned ten pints of brown ale and a chicken korma.
And
too old for punk in the seventies;
I bought the records, not having the nerve to wear
a bumbag or get a mohican;
cos I knew I'd look stupid and
that mohicans had long hair really...
And that 'James Fenimore Cooper'
never bought a single by 'Adam and the Ants'.
But I did.
Furtively
and I played it in secret
while all my chums in the office were

switching on their 'Dire Straits' tapes,
which they exchanged for CDs
as soon as there was a window in their schedules.

Rock and Roll, I gave you the best years of my life.

AN OFFER I CAN'T DEFUSE

She has made me an offer I can't defuse.
Bringing time bombs into a relationship
is just downright irresponsible.
She says it's there merely as a deterrent
to make sure I keep the vows we made.
I say to her,
"How would you like
 it if I brought a cruise missile home?"

My life has become one long nervous tick.

"Darling", I say, "The Bomb is coming between us".
There is no section for Bomb disposal in Yellow Pages,
I phoned the army but they refused to take it,
"You want to be careful with that in your house, sir
there's enough explosive in one of them to level
an entire relationship"

"Dearest" , I say,
 "Does it have to stay in the bedroom at night?
Does it have to have its own macrame hammock?"
I tell her,
"It's no good , I can't, not with 'it' watching.
She goads me, says I'm inadequate.
I lie awake thinking of the opening credits of
'Mission Impossible'.

Sometimes I think of a choice between two wires,
One red, the other blue and in my hand trembling a knife,
I wake up screaming "Red, Red, cut the red!"

But she just smiles and whispers
"But isn't blue a beautiful colour?"

Today, I have taken decisive action.
i have purchased myself a 'bomb'.

it is State-of-the-art,
It has Intel pentium inside and outside.
The man in Dixons had a gleam in his eye
as he whispered 'Kilo-mega-ton'.

and now I know I will have peace in my time,
and now I know my interests are protected
and now I know that the treaty we signed,
the vows that we took, are guaranteed
'Til death us do part'

I have her tea on the table.
I hear her key in the door.
She is expecting lasagne.
But I've prepared a cold war.
I am making an offer she can't defuse.

BAZ AND THE FASCISTS

When Baz stopped bed-wetting
and invited us up to the musty
fantasies of his secret passion
It was like 'Jopling's' window gone mad,
Mannequins kitted out with Nazi regalia.
a primitive arsenal of knives
and crossbows and rice-flails.
Like part of his childhood
got screwed up by the bastard brood
of Bruce Lee and Eva Braun.

One day pissed in Sunderland High Street,
Confronted by some National Front 'skin'
with a copy of 'Bulldog' waving like a flag.
Baz took off his 'dut'
and with rhino-like accuracy
head-butted him to the ground.
and it was poppy day all over the place.

"That's for me Granddad." Baz muttered
moving off in search of new lethal weapons

HOME DEFENSE

Overtaken by paranoia and
the vital need for what the Americans call
'Home Defense'.
i am looking for somewhere to hide
the machete I've just bought from the local
butcher-it-yourself shop.
I find some 'gaffa' tape and
hoist it up snugly under my desk,
testing it out for accessibility,
for ease of swing against some unexpected,
unsuspecting intruder.
i keep it honed to perfection.
It slips as easily as a knife through some nutter.
No one will violate my possessions.
Later in bed, stroking my baseball bat
I contemplate 'hand-to-hand' combat
between myself and a burglar who has discovered
my secret machete. ...... I lose.
I creep cautiously downstairs and exchange
the machete for a swiss army knife I keep in my pyjamas,
and later pondering the wisdom of my actions
bring my entire arsenal to bed.
I contemplate throughout the staircase creaking night,
the options available to me;
Karate courses, Rottweillers,
Burglar alarms, Electric Fences.

I am frightened of the burglar who might have a gun.
I am frightened of the burglar with the psycho friend who
is only made angry by machetes.

I am afraid for my wife and children,
I consider the purchase of automatic weapons for her
and maybe Derringers for the kids.
my wife has sleepless nights
due to my insomnia
She says I should try to close my eyes and rest.
She is frightened for me or maybe of me.
The machete winks in the moonlight.
Maybe I'll buy a shotgun.

In the cold crisp common sense morning,
I unilaterally disarm, stockpile my weapons
for disposal. Telephone freephone insurance.

During the night my car has been stolen.

HE DO THE POLICE IN DIFFERENT VOICES

Policemen are nice people.
I trust them implicitly,
They tell the truth,
the whole truth
and nothing but the truth.
Society is safe in their hands,
Black people are safe in their hands,
Bribes are safe in their hands
and a policemen's lot is
and a policemen's lot is not
and a policemen's lot is not a happy one.

And it's the one bad apple
that spoils the whole blameless barrel
and it's the one sadistic swine
that spoils the whole side of bacon.

And they never over react
or put the boot in or provoke riots
which happen spontaneously
and are inspired by political agitators
and that is not a contradiction
And all political agitators are black or Irish
or in the wrong place at the right time
or the right place at the wrong time,
and confessions are never faked
and the innocent are never imprisoned
and Policemen never get away with murder
and when a felon's not
and when a felon's not engaged
and when a felon's not engaged in his

Unemployment!

Policemen are nice people,
Like Jack Warner, like Charlie Penrose,
like the Keystone Cops, the Bow Street Runners,
Inspector Morse, Spender.
and they're only doing a job
and some one's got to do it,
It's a dirty job but someone's got to do it.

Allo..allo..allo...
It's a fair cop what blows no body no good,
Banged to rights it was society what made me done it.

And the bobby on the beat is as homely as shredded wheat
and if you want to do some time ask a policeman.

THE APATHETIC BLUES

i would go down to the crossroads
if i could be arsed. but my mojo's
not working in fact it's not even
taxed or tested and what with
cigarettes and the hassle of making
your own white lightning..well..
to tell you the truth er....baby
i just don't have the energy or
the inclination to be your hoochie
coochie man. not with this latest
gas bill and the repairs to the roof
and the kids needing new school
uniforms and worst of all..honeychile
i've started writing a twelve bar
called my woman done stayed with me.

THE RACIST NEXT DOOR

me and the racist next door are going out drinking.
celebrating his bigotry, revelling in his intolerance
and when he's drunk enough i am going to kill him.
listen carefully, the racist next door is telling jokes
the one about the 'darkies' the one about the 'gypos'
he is laughing at his own one track wit, but tonight
is his special night, for when he has filled me with
his hatred, i am going to vent his ideology with an axe.

the racist next door with his white smug wife and his
spoilt brat progeny is calling my wife a black bitch.
he's ranting and raving with the full force of his
ordinary level brain, he thinks he is a liberal, he
thinks he is charismatic, he thinks he is superior.
but he doesn't understand my reform, he doesn't
understand, he doesn't understand words like
'dogmatism', he doesn't understand when my wife
calls him an 'arsehole' in bengali. he has no capacity
to comprehend. he thinks being white offers protection.

tonight i will speak to him in his own language
tonight i will converse in a language he will understand,
it is a tongue easily acquired, it is a tongue i used in my
youth.
tonight i will use the linguistics of violence to communicate.
tonight he will learn the colour that we share beneath the
skin.
me and the racist next door are going to paint the town red.

TEN PROBLEMATICAL THINGS TO SAY TO A WOMAN BUS DRIVER ON BOARDING THE SUNDERLAND BUS.

(with apologies to Adrain Mitchell for stealing his wheelbarrow)

1. PATRONISING
If you need any help on the big corners
just give me a shout and I'll be pleased to do it for you,pet.

2. SEXIST
What's a pretty girl like you doing driving on a big bus like this.
It's a shame that they did away with bus conductresses.

3. LECHEROUSLY
I like a woman who can handle big loads.

4. MISGUIDED POLITICALLY CORRECT.
You have a perfect right to drive this bus.
I shall enjoy this as much, if not more
than a similar journey with a driver
of the opposing gender.

5.HOMOPHOBICALLY
There's no reason why a lesbian such as
yourself can't do the job as well
as a 'normal' person.

6.METAPHYSICALLY
Mighty are the bus stops of the soul
and you are the Amazonian charioteer
of Time's winged chariot.

7.INFORMATIVELY
During wartime many women drove buses

and indeed ambulances and other public utility vehicles. Ultimately leading to a post-war discontent amongst women as a work force. Historically this has proved to be of lasting consequence and a positive factor in the battle for equality and emancipation.
Oh and do you stop outside of Asda?

8.MYSOGYNISTICALLY
Carry on madam. I shall wait for the
next conveyance which has a man at the wheel.

9. MARXIST
This red bus is a metaphor for the unending class struggle and this exchange of money between myself and yourself will inevitably lead to the fall of the bourgeoisie capitalist state and thus the creation of a new world order!

10. LIBERAL APOLOGETICALLY
I have nothing against women drivers .
Don't get me wrong, some of my best friends are women.

However, in my experience
the best thing to say upon boarding a bus driven by a woman
is ; £3.20 return to Sunderland, please.

SKID MARKS ON THE ANTI-MACASSAR

A lost key and splintered woodwork.
Coffee without milk or sugar,
Dog-ends from choked ashtrays.
Fist-marks on plywood doors.
Threadbare carpets and cracked crockery.
A found coin for light and heat.
Red bills gathering like clans.
One ring left on an electric cooker.
Dead geraniums on a sunless window sill.
Two crusts in a metal bread bin.
Cold peas from a tin with a stolen spoon.
Books by candlelight in a nylon sleeping bag.
Breathing out plumes in a freezing room.
Stolen silver from an old red phone box.
The smell of condoms on your fingers.
Lust and lager in a cold climate.
Skid marks on the Anti-macassar.

THE BOLSHEVIK EDGE

Mayakovsky got it right,
put a bullet in it
before it got out of control
and between
blood and women,
chose blood.

In the Rosta windows
drawing workers with
his eyes closed,
swollen fingers
muffled against the cold.

"We don't need a dead temple of art
where dead works languish, but a
living factory of the human spirit"

The hammer bends the sickle
the wheels that forged motion
grind to memoirs of revolution.
Mayakovsky got it right,
After all this time.

Buying chic bolshevism
from galleries, the
blood of Mayakovsky
on a thousand different
walls.

A GUINEA PIG CALLED CHOCOLATE

and a rabbit whose name I can't remember.
lived peacefully in the converted chest of drawers.
ate the dandelion leaves and mare's tail
ate the cabbages and the cauliflowers
ate the food we gathered for them;
dock and chick-weed and plantain.
ate the scraps of carrots and turnip
from the Sunday dinner.
ate the milk and cereal and biscuits
we made them,
ate anything and everything
even the rhubarb leaves
which killed them.

their bodies stiff and fake
in natural taxidermy,
like lovers
or religious fanatics
in a death pact.
slivers of blood
on bloated tongues.

THE LEGEND OF THE INDIAN PRINCE

Dad said that Indian Prince was the best tea ever,
Dad said that if Indian Prince had been a soldier
it would have won the Victoria Cross and lived.
Dad said if Indian Prince had been a footballer
it would have been Stanley Matthews, Eusebio
Pele and Michael Owen all rolled into one,
Dad said if Indian Prince hadn't of been a packet of tea
it probably would have become Prime Minister.
Dad said that if Indian Prince had been a squirrel
it would have evolved opposing thumbs and
developed its own civilisation.
Dad said that if Indian Prince had been an explorer
it would have circumnavigated the world
single handedly, twice.
Dad said that Indian Prince was better than all the
teacups in China.
Dad said the best way to make tea, son is
to go to the Co-op, buy a packet of Indian Prince,
sit in front of the telly and get someone else to
make it for you!
Dad said that if Indian Prince had been a popstar
it would have Elvis Presley or the Beatles or
The artist formerly known as Indian Prince!

Dad said too much about tea.
When Dad died, Mam bought PG tips
and the man in the Co-op said,
I drink Indian Prince and I'll tell you why,
Because Indian Prince is the Lord of the Leaves,
Indian Prince is the Maharajah of Char,

If Indian Prince hadn't of been a packet
of tea I would have settled down and
had children with it.
He was as daft as my Dad!

My luv is like a brown, brown brew
that tastes as good e'en when it's stewed

I am the product of decades of tea drinkers,
I have measured out my life in teaspoons.
My ancestors are all as straight as tea bags
But I prefer coffee.

If Indian Prince had been my Father
it would be spinning in its grave.

BAZ AND THE FREEDOM OF THE PRESS

Full of Hell,
Baz gatecrashes the chip-shop,
bringing down on the counter a greasy
newspaper, bearing a colour image
of a topless model.

"It's a fucking disgrace, you should
watch what you're selling,
I bought them chips for my little girl"

The chip-shop owner is
caught somewhere between
bemused and terrified and
pours two lots of vinegar
on some wifie's tail-end.

He stutters meekly,
"But..but.. I only sell chips!"

Baz rumbles on about guards in Auschwitz
and then explodes,
"Bloody typical,
I bet you're a Tory,
Only a bloody Tory rag
would print this filth
and only a Tory would
wrap up my little girl's chips
in pornography.

"But....but.."

The chip-shop queue
are nodding their agreement
and checking their wrappings
for nudes.

The poor bastard is sweating now
and apologising, he offers Baz
a free Fish and Chip lunch.
Baz graciously accepts the offer.
The queue warmly applauds his exit.

Outside I remind Baz
that he hasn't got a little girl
and he reminds me
who's got the free lunch.

COLD SPELL

In cold January
when the snow
made our joints ache
we built a snow woman
to keep the peace.

and now the two
stand
side by side,
snow man and snow woman
and our little girl
is the power
that no man
may put asunder.

although later
and forlorn in thaw,
the marriage of the two
has been dissolved